Moveable Type
Rommi Smith

route

First Published in 2000 by Route
School Lane, Glasshoughton, West Yorks, WF10 4QH
e-mail: books@route-online.com

ISBN: 1 901927 11 3

Editor: Ian Duhig
Cover Design: Andy Campbell & Dean Smith
Cover Image: Kevin Reynolds
Support: Ian Daley, Clayton Devanny, Nicole Devlin, Dean Smith

Special Thanks to:
Lynda Plummer for belief and inspiration from the start
Julie Darwood for words and wishbones
Ian Duhig for crucial support, encouragement and sharing wisdom
And to libraries everywhere!

Printed by Cox and Wyman, Reading

A catalogue for this book is available from the British Library

Full details of the Route programme of books
and live events can be found on our website
www.route-online.com

Route is the fiction imprint of YAC, a registered charity No 1007443

YAC is supported by
Yorkshire Arts, West Yorkshire Grants, Wakefield MDC,
Arts Council of England

Contents

For my mother and sister, as promised.
and as always, with much love.

The hebrew for compass,
is the same word for conscience

Daniel Gross (1999)
English Hebrew Dictionary
Hippocrene Books, New York

Acknowledgements

These poems have been performed on BBC radio and television, ITV, Channel Four, at music and literature festivals through out the UK and internationally at venues that include the University of Madrid, the Nuyorican Poets Cafe and the Tribes Gallery in New York.

The poem Red was comimissioned by Barnardo's as part of its World AIDS Day awareness campaign.

Justice for Joy is an extract from the poetry narration written for the docu-film *Sieze The Time,* broadcast on Channel Four.

The poems *The Something Seeker, Clock Watching* and *Home* were comisioned by Leeds City Voice Literature Festival as part of a text and dance site-specific piece of theatre. The piece, *All The Way Home,* premiered at Leeds City Station and explored the issue of discrimination towards refugees.

Salted Grin was written during my time as writer-in-residence for *Support and Survival,* a Wakefield based project, supporting women who are living with, or escaping domestic violence.

Mother: Daughter was commisioned by Leeds City Voice Festival and premiered at the West Yorkshire Playhouse in Leeds.

Love Song Lyric Blues is taken from the play *Angie Baby* commissioned by Paines Plough Theatre Company.

Foreword

Brodsky wrote of poetry as the song of the nomad as against the prose of the farmer and that is an insight at the heart of this collection. The essentially musical nature of poetry is here addressed in the writing as well as the accompanying CD, for Rommi Smith has taken care to ensure that her poems stand up on the page as well as on stage, where she is a renowned performer. Structurally, this is reflected in the cyclical elements of the book and its skilfully-developed imagery of travel, identity and language. It also employs imagery from nature, but this is double edged: the homeless and emigrants are exposed to its moods and brutality in a way that the settled, dominant society is not. But although the traditional strengths of the craft here work to great effect, Rommi Smith binds her means and meanings together, and her writing makes important political points. For all the apparent affluence of contemporary England and America, many of those excluded from the feast by previous governments are still going hungry; for all the vaunted liberalism, racist organizations grow and racist murder is a fact of our lives.

Valerie Bloom has written 'the writer who happens to be black is expected to be the voice of black people in a way the writer who is white is not.' Rommi Smith rises to this challenge as to all others. She is one of a growing band of contemporary poets who press wit and accomplishment into work which deals with the major issues of today. This book establishes her as one of its leading members.

Ian Duhig

TLC Street

There's a man who's falling for life
on the red carpet pavement of TLC Street.
There's a wealth ploughed in his face
but no mirrored fortune is found in his pockets.

An NBC camera ships these songs to its public
on a label called Tragic,
there's a woman who carries her voice in her Gaultier bag
but, she's yearning to sing.

At the subway turnstile a woman seeks shut eye
on top of an electrical box;
home-goers sneak preview
the craftwork of her
worldly possessions tied up in knots.
They mouth disgust at delay. The red tape of rush hour:
'How many stops before home is this?'
She's an exhibit on full view
but she's no exhibitionist.

How tender hearts
get the sharp shoulder,
and love and care
walk arm in arm like the ghosts of war soldiers,
past the brusque
and the grazed
on TLC Street.

There's a family in a four-door
on the corner of Caught Emotion
on TLC Street.
Where the grime and glamour
vie for honour,

on TLC Street.
They watch Big Life on the small screen
of the rear view mirror,
counting ring can pull silver,
king of the castle, on a car-seat throne,
the headlamps are on, but no one is home,
the future's a thought to sleep on, though,
when the end of the rainbow is
the end of the road.
There's a mother
who keeps moments
in a locket
like a compass for home:
a reminder.

There's a brother
with news in a letter
in the breast of his jacket
and he's yearning for home.
Mere mortals turn godly for Justice;
'How many prayers before change is this?'
There's faith on the block, but who cares to notice?

How tender hearts
get the sharp shoulder,
and love and care
walk arm in arm like the ghosts of war soldiers,
past the brusque
and the grazed
on TLC Street.

Mother: Daughter

Mother's voice in bold, Daughter's voice in normal print

I came from her
her pointed features
her pale skin,
I visit no mirror
to ask for her
offering.

It's in the eyes,
gesture, jawline:
pieces of
my jigsaw, emerging.

I ease stories from her
like babies
to map out her history
before me:

We met in the 1960s
we chain-smoked parties
arm in arm, we would
walk down a city street
in our mouths - ignorance;
on the inside our hearts beat
de-fi-ance.
I felt like we'd bit parts from
High Chapparal,
where the baddies or
the guys from out of town
walk in,
and the in-crowd
goldfish-mouthed,
stop drinking.

Except she constructed make believe
being gawped at meant
the status of royalty,
one spectator's dirty bucket of water
was just liquid confetti;
and love, love is thicker than water.

By the skin of your neck
I dragged you through the alphabet
to repeat words
discover them
and I never
let you forget.

Each word a witness
of the journey to tell:
one more knot in
the elephant's tail.

Just
when I
thought
that the
motion
of the train
was a successful
lullaby -
the old lady leans over
her inquisitive finger
confirming her intrigue
like they were exotic confectionery,
my baby dolls,
my little girls,
she casts a wry eye
over my whiteness,

their brownness,
and confesses everything.

Identity was deemed to be
one thing or the other
and blackness
always seemed
to mean
disremembering
my mother.

The brutal currency of playground exchange
was construed as quips she 'couldn't take',
'half –breed'
'semi-nigger'
'bounty bar'
said,
for her to be left
with 'Eenie, meenie, minie, mo'
as the tail between her legs.

Identity was deemed to be
one thing or the other
and blackness
always seemed
to mean
disremembering
my mother.

Gloria is a talker,
at work her tongue cleans the corners of childhood
mine remains firmly behind the wood work.
She says, her front room fascist husband
is just misunderstood.
Me and my daughters

meet them aisle trudging
on their family outing
to find his food.

Her tongue is sinew round her husband's
little finger,
I didn't look the sort
to have such daughters,
their judging eyes can't look any deeper
and nasty silence doesn't hide
its truth.

She taught me that there
had to be a way
out of no way,
that courage
mustn't make
a fleeting visit
and that strength
for life
is a pre-requisite.

Identity
was
deemed
to be
one place
or the other
and Blackness
always seemed
to mean
disremembering mother.

The Love Song Lyric Blues

'Poems are other people's photographs in which we recognise ourselves'.
Charles Simic

I'm on first name terms with those who take such care as they
sing my biography; Aretha, Dusty, Dionne, Chaka, Shirley, Patsy.
Legends of my record player.
Maidens of this salt-streak-faced community;

'There, now, there',
crying seas, not rivers,
everywhere.

It happened quietly, quickly.
One hum too many of 'you don't have to say you love me',
next minute my tent of self-esteem gave in.

Torrents of 'don't it make my brown eyes blue', turned tent to
float, through flattened shanty towns called 'promises, promises'
down the sheer surfaces of 'ain't no mountain high enough'
patterned with 'careless whispers'. I spat these stones from a
borrowed language:

'hey little girl comb your hair fix your make-up', 'to hold you,
build my world around you' 'wear your hair just for him' 'loving
you the way I do, I'd take you back, without you I'd die, dear'.
'I've got to stay true just, as long as he needs me'

I spat these stones of ice
I sang spent wishes
I'd sung an igloo before
I'd finished,
filed for bankruptcy at the Home Office,
owed Bacharach and David royalties.

I clung on,
was lost and found
in an off-track town
near Sanity
just short of
a place named
'I would give everything I own'
then realised -
my oars
were arguments
I'd left at home,

a bathroom's warble
became my normal voice.
My tune, a red herring, a lonely choir
rode on, rose out of steam.
Glory. Hubris. Valhalla.

I picked up style.
at Tescos,
at the delicatessen
I stood -
asked for
half a pound of ham
like Shirley Bassey
on at the Palladium, would.

I started quoting
Smokey Robinson, like a
demon – 'through the tracks of
my tears' 'didn't care
about anything else but
being with you,
being with you'

Oooh.
Ooooh.
Oooooh.

'One day at a time, sweet Jesus'
one fist 'hanging on the telephone'.
til 'the tears of a clown '
had become my own.

A thousand days and nights
a thousand lines of
mass-produced advice,
revolving round the deck
aflame; sure of voices
to light the way
for Jude, the Saint
of Lost Causes.

Each story deals the
same card:
this turntable -
my Scheherazade.

I mistook for love, notes
plucked from grooves
that silk-strip memory
to misery. Until I understood
that 'standing by your woman,
or man', is an unwise move
in the path of a train
that signing up to
'never love again'
Is a tad premature
in the warmth of next day.

A full-time diva
with a part-time soul,
seeks a lyric for escape
and with tracks as her backbone -
it seems that
one exit's Nashville
and the other Motown.

A Touch of the Old Plath and Hughes

Dave is down in the sunny South,
Alice thinks rosy is the answer.
Dave's lined up the ships in full sail,
but he can't find the way to the harbour.

Once they were childhood jam,
now they're not even chinas.
Dave said: 'home's gale, not whale',
so he sailed away
over the fisherman's daughter.

Bessie Smith's Blues

Whose red voice
rides the spinning wheel for truths?
Who takes the brunt of blunt regard, yet moves? -
Well, it's the legend of your record player
shining her torch song blues.

Notes spark the stars to slumber, for a time
a slice of lemon hangs in the sky;
well it's a rock-a-bye baby
for this sweet woman and I.

The Empress of Blues, listed wishes:
to sing, a wad of green bills; a red dress for a lover to live in
a Pullman for escape
and a glass of bath-tub gin.

A motherless child sinks a glass of mother's ruin,
a tin bath and a landscape of dark skin.
Landscape lit by moonshine. Lives lit by singing.

A tune with an alphabet of bitter language.
A thwarted hope on the tongue of the definitive.
One step for progression,
two footprints backwards.

Those lost hours the doctors thought no-one would miss
it took seven hours to be stitched up, and the point is this:
it seems that Route 16
just amounts to Route 6,6,6.

Shine a torch with your voice, Bessie
put the stars to the test.
Shine a torch with your voice, Bessie
put the moon out to rest,
as the mouth of your car
travels unexpectedly west.

The Something Seeker

Memory is shady. Milky. Cocoa?
Sleep dear, the present is ghastly.
You are a nomad in your own city;
its circumstance carves you.
You stare through an album of shop windows,
butcher, baker, tracing emotions the elements echo.
Fresh air? A walk in sharp rain, cleaner?
Rain, only washes desire clearer.
You'd cry if you had but a handkerchief,
you'd ring out grief for all its sentiment.
Here, where the streets swapped stars for sulphur,
a clock ticks backwards; tows the episodes of years.
Laughter. A hollow soul's running on relief.
Far from empty. Distance is purely a magnifier.
Only you know where you are.
The lights have died above the chemists' shop.
You sought the antidote.
Out of luck.
Walls stripped bare.
Shutters down.
Living happened elsewhere.

Houdini

It's a sink or swim feeling,
the paddle, a pick,
the stream, one of numbers
the First Amendment
the float under him.

Or, it's one cloud of breath
left in the mouth, in a tank
made of brick, to the rim
with illusion. Or was that Baptism? -
Marked like a witness, provided the answers.

Then, it's the image of him
turning his back on the games,
palaver, commotion, routine,
Regulation -
now this is the name on the jumpers
he's wearing

Next, the hangman on the face of a card
then a prayer for insurance,
luck, or fair weather.
In the head – there's one magpie
in the heart, he's the mayor,
with the keys to the city
pouring milk on his freedom,
his tongue, the scissors
that cut the red ribbon.

Clock Watching

Clock watching –
time grows
waiting to welcome my lover home
to be reacquainted with
warm tones
now distant
to the raucousness of the children
circling the station in screams.

A statement of flowers and a brief case
of longing, it's been but few days
but I'm yearning
to match the voice to the face, again.

The tannoy system
a day dream breaker
announcing shuffled time
to destinations
to off-beat,
on-track railway stations.

The soft low, swing high
of sweet somethings on
the nearest mobile phone,
brings it all back to me
sings me into reality.

Home

One refugee
swallowed emotion,
barraged the backdoor.
Prayed. Snapped a wishbone.
Sang songs for justice
avoided the telephone,
as one refugee went all the way home.

One refugee was respected with integrity
to be who they were -
they joined a community
carved a place
in the
lap of the city
but one refugee went all the way home.

One refugee
handed their past in
at the Customs and Excise:
'Anything for
declaring?'
'My name, my country
my reason for leaving'
as one refugee went all the way home.

One refugee started a campaign
for words, action, wisdom
and humility again,
built petitions
a vision of the way,
as another refugee went all the way home

One refugee knocked at the inn,
the beds weren't to spare
there were
nowt for the taking,
accused of squealing, scrounging
and faking
so one refugee went all the way home.

One refugee took on the big wigs,
pin-stripe suits dealing fortune cookie justice
as a reminder
from Survivors
from the places on these lips,
to those marking time for who can't and who can:

Belsen
Biafra
Uganda
Cambodia
Kosovo
Auschwitz
Chile
Sudan.

Red

Once Red
was just
the flesh
of ribbon
in her hair
the neckline of
swimwear.
Now it shifts
from halter
to hook-line
to noose round the neck.

Truth is the
Red sharp
of snakes' tongues
that spikes
the heart
of fearmongers' whispers
spilling their bleach onto content of character.

Remembrance of Red
was once
just
the post-box red
of a lipstick gash
on a first-date mouth.

Years later,
Red marks the date stamp
the frankness of the letter:
decisions on doormats
and futures on paper.

These are Red times.

Red.

The last wine stains on the carpet
after painting the town.

Red.

The hands of wall climbing children
Inpatient to be grown.

Red,

was simply the symbol for
new life.

Plush petal
cut stem
charting the journey
from girl through to woman
now it's the shade of a
well-kept song
played
on
and
on
and
on.

Across a Crowded Gym...

It's the middle of rush hour in this gym
my mind is dancing with the rhythm of
Adrenaline Evangelicals
pumping fantasy
on the backs of machines.

Knowing
they'll have all the charm of a shot putter with a
tricep injury,
I cross the carriageway
to the changing room
to slip into something more comfortable like

my own identity.

I'm working my way past a tailback of egos
reaching the junction between
Body Pump and cardiac arrest
through the queue for the Bench Press Confessional

I'm looking to find you.

Against the back drop of the video screen
Desire marks 4/4 time by the light of MTV.
Across the landscape of sweat that becomes our sea,
portable speakers filter mortal angel's voices.

This is déjà vu
I have loved you
before in another exercise class was it -
Yoga, or Salsa Aerobics?

Somewhere, some place,
near the virtual ski run
that's where they'll find us
You are lips, hips. I'm all
teeth and trainers.

Like Olivia Newton John
we're 'getting physical' with
Nike and Helly Hanson on
whilst Dedicated Followers of Flagolation
check the heart monitor for a murmur of emotion
work up crocodile perspiration
notch up the calorific value of bravado.

You are ice-cream for these warm nights.
This is intimacy under strip light.
Are we alone with the horizon
of introspective sets of eyes,
set tight in the heads of those jogging to oblivion?

We will waltz amongst these wrought machines,
as the six-pack crew pant
the soundtrack to the action.

The lullabies
of Personal Trainers,
will gently
carry
us
home.

Moveable Type

Her father threw
a cast-iron typewriter
at her mother's head, and
missed.

That day
her mother left.

It's unmistakable
the imprint on the wall
the impact sent the coiled ribbons reeling.

Stewn blues and reds
carriage lop sided, arse-over-tit
in a messed up muddled heap in the hallway
as her mother, so easily could have been.

The stark space bar - a statement,
an empty back row
whose kissers walked out in the interval.

The dent
of a new sentance
a bruised cheek of metal-
teeth of alphabet keys
spelling it out on the lino.

The noise of indentation
surely earmarked for discussion, yet
the zipped mouths of neighbours
remained knowingly clueless as to
the source.

Last impressions last.
Torn Vymura, the silt of anger -
the shattered, powdered plaster
beneath unfulfilled prayers
seemed only marked
'Return to Sender.'

The light may have been on
but no-one was home.

The light may have been on
but no-one was home.

New York

We are rubbernecking the city sights,
feeling like rednecks
out on the town
for the first time.
Carrying the relic of our Englishness,
staring at phallic skyscrapers built
with pieces from a Tycoon's Lego set:
Chrysler, Vanderbilt or Trump?

Only rich blokes get by with names like that.

On the silver-streaked capsules of the subway system
city-suits practise self- imposed autism
whilst boys with Houdini's vision,
the square root of their mothers' ages
between them,
beatbox and sing about
'Lovin' you girl';
precision timed
to last the duration
between each station stop,
just enough of the novelty left
to ask for dimes in their McDonald's box.

¿Que es esta contradicción?
¿Por qué lo amo?

The New York Police building
flashes its authority in brothel neon
theatrically viewing crime rates
with Broadway as its spine,
so is it showdown
or is it show time?

¿Que es esta contradicción?
¿Como puedo amarlo?

Streets sponsored by MTV
Madonna Lane
and Sinatra Street
compliments the 'wealth of the free';
nails by Macy's
blank face by Magritte.

Street sleepers tucked up on concrete,
dog crèches and dog boutiques,
whilst Public Access Theatre offers
Macbeth free,
in Central Park

¿Que es esta contradicción?
¿Como puedo amarlo?

And this energy just pelts through the city
like dodgy traffic
on pedestrian walk ways?
Whilst Joni Mitchell sings
ecologically
about the pitfalls of big yellow taxis.

There's a parking lot
where there was once greenery.

The leaf, the seed, the wood,
is oiled over by machinery.
And nothing that could come to any good
is anywhere to see.
And nothing that could come to any good
is anywhere to see.

But parking lots hold those big yellow taxis
the glitzless
get rich,
short cut
pauper's limousines.
The leaves that grow,
it's hoped,
are wads in wallets.
When certainty states that
dreams don't grow on trees.

When certainty states that
dreams don't grow on trees.

When certainty states that
dreams don't grow on trees.

We are rubbernecking the city sights,
feeling like rednecks
out on the town
for the first time.
Carrying the relic of our Englishness,
staring at phallic skyscrapers built
with pieces from a tycoon's Lego set:
Chrysler, Vanderbilt or Trump?

Only rich blokes get by with names like that.

Me and Ainsley Harriot on Broadway

Broadway
12 o clock
midnight
Starbucks' coffeeshop
Ainsley Harriot
in the door way
by the moonlight.

I came here to find Madonna
and Lauryn Hill in a cafe corner;
eggs – easy over,
pancakes and chowder,
instead it's
me and Ainsley Harriot on Broadway.

No
he didn't
ask me to empty the items in my bag,
inspect them,
rustle up a meal for two
in a few seconds.

Didn't take a Scotch Bonnet
from under his Panama
set my plate on fire
and say, 'Voilà'.

Nor did he
serve fellow diners
a top-tip
on how to slice an onion correctly with
the sharp edge of gossip.

I came here to find
rappers from the East and West Coast,
Scott Joplin's
Maple Leaf Rag
served over Melba Toast,
instead it's me and Ainsley Harriot on Broadway.

No way did he approach me
uttering the catchphrase
tender, firm, and juicy.

He didn't wield a whisk
like a wand and flick the lights -
slip into something
more comfortable -
like chef whites.

He did nothing of the sort,
he didn't dare
we could have been Ginger Rogers and Fred Astaire
tripped the light fantastic
schlepped debonair
whilst
Bessie Smith
sipped on Blue Notes.

I smiled at Ainsley
he looked none the wiser,
he was a tv chef in New York
I was the stranger.

No 42nd Street wide smile
depressingly ordinary -
He was a tv chef in New York.
He was on holiday.

I came here to find
Mickey Mouse in Times' Square
handing out family fun,
Will Smith
on the ferry to Staten Island
Letterman and Rivers
sharpening their tongues.
Instead it's me and Ainsley Harriot on Broadway.

Summary of a Late Night American Chat Show

(after Sophie Hannah's poem A Summary of a Western)

A wide angle bird's eye shot,
a roaring crowd
and that's
the way the ordeal begins.
Some triple-timing-rat
delivers a Pandora's Box
to fame fresh faces,
robs a trained counsellor
of brand new cases,
tempts the newly troubled to trip over their laces.

'Exs' meet 'presents', meet 'futures'
on stage and power naked hosts lap up their rage.
It means the highest ratings in the land
who sleeps with whom
we don't quite understand,
there's always soapbox statements like
'He's my man.'

Etiquette of conversation thwarted,
fisticuffs and bloodshed are rewarded,
the deletion of 'f' words provides an interesting rhythm,
steroid enhanced bouncers delay intervention,
the self-righteous audience shares insults with the nation.

Women in negligées are to be distrusted,
gender is deceptive,
love deemed oppressive,
closet viewers feign ignorance
of this new psychosis
saying
that the reason that they watch it is,
to cure insomnia
and for research purposes.

Mrs Cherry

A response to the DfEE campaign to recruit more people into the teaching profession.

Cherry pie. Cherry Blossom.
Cherry cake. Cherry red.

Mrs Cherry.

The heavy door slams,
BANG!
Quick, like amoeba,
she splits, holds her
politeness to parents ransom,
quits any knowledge of her
name's association.

Cane thin. Her frame, a wick
of tunic green, her pristine
sugar starched collar
in a rash of multicolour
is supposed to indicate
her frivolous sense of humour.

Underneath
all this terse,
the well-versed seductress
has another side.

Our hours were filled with games of
hide and seek for pairs of scissors -
up her sleeve.
False starts for the
home time,
the break time

the lunchtime queues,
drilled with words,

'I didn't tell you to go
you weren't supposed to.'

Mrs Cherry,
the fickle friend of the 'five year old'.
Her ill-will smothered in birthday treats,
shop cakes, bought only for deserving class mates
who stood in a juvenile, gibbering
Maundy Service queue.

Mrs Cherry: the dentist's apprentice,
armed with cup cakes
and charisma,
knowing a fix of sugar
will coat a put-down,
or the full beast of her terror.

Mrs Cherry
Beelzebub's accomplice,
Mary Poppins with
malice in her sandwiches.

She earmarked me aged five,
I tried to do an 'Olga Corbett' back flip.
'Nul point.'
So, she knicked my wounded pride
with the whisper: 'I knew you couldn't.'

Next the accusation that I spat
for which I was forced to sit outside without a jam-jar
told –'Fill it!'
A child's eternity later,
back, sheepish, tearstained

quest incomplete, with a rat-a-tat-tat
on the old wooden door
like, Red Riding asking
the wolf to let her in?

She chatised my lack of enterprise
without relent,
God
I couldn't even fulfil the requirements
of punishment.

If she could see me now,
my patent leather shoes
are now, booted size eights,
I'd ignore the sign on the door
that says:

Knock and wait.
Knock and wait.

But should I - salvage my spit from the sill
that she's been using as a mark
of her power?
Substitute it for the milk in her tea
saying 'Drink, drink, in remembrance of me.'

Or subject her to reading my full CV
in a style of my choosing.
Or, just simply, in mild silence,
write her mantra on the board
and like a snake eats
its tale,
she'll consume
her own words -

see,
I knew you couldn't.

The Trace of James Brown's Scream

There's an A and R executive
paid to interrogate every
Big Smoke, small town, play-list
for the sound of James Brown's scream.

She specialises in
sifting scores
tapping the fine line of a groove
with her bureaucratic fingertips,
checking for the borrowed crust of soul
sandwiched between new tunes
bathed in infancy, christened by
the Godfather, unwittingly.

She defines the sliding scale,
calculates the cost
of a silver string of 'get on ups'.

Brands the L,T,D and C
to the TM and thus royalties.

There is no question of her
'picking up' her 'bad self'
in the morning, the afternoon, or even the evening,
to end up acting like a 'sex-machine'
without a few nickels
in the 'money-maker'
or a stock up on 'soul power'
a little while later.

Meanwhile,
Mr Brown is singing through his bars
and adjusting his scales,
the figures are rising
and he's getting paid

Well it's the
sharp-toothed
soul-mouthed truth
that licks the roof of law.

His screams are on commission,
his wife's — unaccounted for.

Read My Palms, This Is Being Alive

Then, it's the simple things, this
making sense of skin. We
photograph this moment
for posterity.

The moon that midnight
possesses,
is the the glint of a rim
of a trumpet horn.

Look how far we've come.
Well-kept our words: silence wakes a deeper subject.
A look is a whisper of cream to an earlobe.
Touch. A found language. Morse code on finger-tips.

Now, a small part of the heart, still reserved,
for reunion, marked as sold. Out of bounds.
Caught time. The past is the comfort of a known
hand. So, here. Take mine.

Justice for Joy

i.m. of Joy Gardener

Q. How many police officers and deportation official does it take to murder a Black woman?

A. None according to the British Criminal Justice System

Q. How does thirteen feet of tape make its way around the head of another human being?

A. As if by magic according the British Criminal Justice System?

Q. What can happen to police officers, who break into a home, ransack the place. Break into a home and mask the face of a woman who was disturbed from sleep with her son?

A. Nothing according to the British Criminal Justice System

Take the word murder with a capital M,
with a body-belt and leg irons and add to all of them
hand-cuffs and thirteen feet of tape.
I feel my smile turn to tears and my anger turn to hate.
You know I realised what makes Britain
really ain't that great, so don't
cover my eyes to the truth and don't try to deceive me,
when they say that shackles went out with slavery.

'But Joy Gardener, she wasn't British'
I hear Bernard Manning from the back,
damn if it's that, it's just she was Black.

Do you remember the name
Amadou Diallo?
Do you remember the name
Kwenale Siziba?
Do you remember the name
Stephen Lawrence?

So don't cover my eyes to the truth
and don't try to deceive me.
It is a damn, damn shame and it's damn
hypocrisy that the very institution that should protect us
are a law unto themselves,
we are left on our own
and we know where we stand
and it leaves nothing else.

There has been no justice for Joy.
She did not have the opportunity to challenge
Bobby McFerrin
as to who the hell he was addressing
when he said that the safe attitude to take
of all people world–wide was,
'don't worry, be happy.'

Joy, you know your death
is the salute
to signal the silence to them singing
Land Of Hope And Glory as
Jack-a-nory.
Pure Jack-a-nory.

You were told the streets were paved with gold,
you found the tin underneath.
You ain't never found the gold
but you just found the grief.
And there should be no rest
and there should be no peace
with the bigoted state and the prejudiced police

until there is justice for Joy.
Until there is justice for Joy.
Until there is justice for Joy.

Paper Ships

And once again we find ourselves, here
at the summit.

You: making delicate
origami paper ships
from frustation and
flourescent discount entry leaflets-
to clubs we won't visit.

Me: playing pyrotechnics with a box
of in-house matches.

The table is the bridge
under a naked sea of conversation
the people, the happy soundtrack
to the reconciliation of our empty glasses.

You: mending the transparent view
with obstacles
me: threatening to sail off into that
seductive night,
that we both
want to walk
home through.

Perfect Teeth

The view from the concrete harbour
was spectacular.
Crescents of white teeth. Suitcases marked Past Lives.
Hands raised to wave.

It was sometime later though,
I realised that they were reaching for
something beyond the frame.

A fragment of those who've journeyed from the dock
where you can't recast a tremor
as a ripple
or call it love.

The Great Escape

'I perceived as I read' – *The Autobiography of Malcolm X*

'A world that is a book is devoured by a reader who is a letter in
the world's text'.- Alberto Manguel – *A History of Reading*.
Flamingo (1997)

1

The slammer, the cells, the lock-up
a stretch in the nick with screws for comfort.
There's a wind outside and he'd be peeing into it
except for the brick wall, the bucket.
No sand, or spade
but an audience.
Marks out of ten for the height and the gradient,
the arc of the stream of golden showers.
The heart is hopeful:
the mind is porridge

11

This is a blue moon.

The doctor's instructions state
take one at a time
dissolve round the mind slowly,
sparcely, spearingly, at first, then
increase the dosage when
ready. Take at regular intervals
complete the course, but
return anything unused –
to the Library.

111

Four green stubs in the sweat of a palm
which christens them nicely,
marks the start of the journey
one line in
it's like he's never been away.

And didn't he have a luverly time
the day he went to Oz, Gormenghast, Toy-town, Narnia,
all for the price of a palm crossed with paper.
A bird in the hand is worth two on the roof.

1111

The alphabet -
vinegar and brown paper for his head,
which like a miracle
flip turns
the word
slammer
to bearable,
each tongue wrapped round a strange vowel
A and E: IOU
to warm the articifial night
to make the morning edible.

Morning will find him
quietly overdosing
on a dictionary
in a picturesque part of the library,
the old pleasure and pain, begins to
tick again, begin again
his freedom - words
his sentence - medicine.

Red Shoes

Faith
was the realisation
that speaking truth
wouldn't turn milk poison,
that there was life on the doorstep as
well as the pint of milk.

Friends' ice-pack hearts began to thaw,
tested too often,
too much,
too raw,
and it's a humble pain
when you're inside
with a mind dressed for rain.

So she
etched out a new plan A,
fixed for years,
tongue-tied time finds the words,
just move.

If you
brave blank ground
you wield a wise soul;
you brood
you lose
so discard map pass
go.

Hedge bets
that brute hope won't save dead dreams,
don't
look
back.
Race on,
flag up,
glance 'bye!'
at the ghost of a patchwork
patched life.

Grace your soul in no-one's hands
just believe.
Make pact, sort out
from rubbished, rubble mess.

Ahead,
yellow brick road,
red shoes
on west.

Ahead,
yellow brick road,
red shoes
on
west.

Ahead,
yellow brick road,
red shoes
on
west.

Scarecrow

Well here I am
with one straight leg,
I pirouette.
A trained
constrained
ballet dancer?
A jewel box miniature -
a cracked tinny music mover?

Watch my weather worn
mock dainty spin,
my smile's diamante
emotions'
auctioned off for charity.

Who planted me here
so that vines
could claim status as the veins in my legs?
You, I expect.

Left, with only wilderness
as my accomplice
til my fingers
sussed the wind's
intent,
grew shears
redeemed
freedom.
No further expense.

How does it feel gardener
to come back to the plot
where you simply forgot you
had planted me?
And see a hole and a stake
where your former adornment
should be?

Salted Grin

Dedicated the users of Women's AID and Support and Survival
Inspired by the traditional song – He Moved Through The Fair

My young love
said to me
there's a slice of the moon that's a piece of cheese
and like the fox to the crow, said
you'll swallow it whole, if you're able.

You can kneel to face grief
in a stream that's a mirror,
you can kiss your reflection
in pursuit for better,
but water keeps distance
that words try to meet, if they ever.

And he moved through the fair
the pretty, the sage,
like a Jack Frost tapping
on each tender window pane
dared to give my qualities as gifts to strangers
then said for me to
hang myself on his ribbonesque lips,
if I cared to.

Yes he stepped away from me
with a snatch at the sky, he has
bartered stars for pennies
and drunk cellars dry.
He has slung the sun a promise
in the hope it won't shine
now there's one star left to pluck
from the blank night.

Last night he came to me, he came softly in
outside, rain was falling like a prediction,
and he was
whispering blue seduction through
his salted grin, whilst
his rum stung fingers leaked an omen.

I learnt how the shadow of a kiss
is just a stopper for light
how it ignites a tongue to
stub out a mind.

My queue to start walking
you're thinking? I hear you.
But his tongue is a spindle
that's weaving this warning -
how the door is the size
of the frame of my coffin,
how the door is the size
of the frame of my coffin.

The Invitation

The sight:
almost a biblical story.
Jamaica to Tilsbury's harbour,
an ark sailing without a Noah,
ship steel instead of Moses
parting the waters,
fuelled by the promise
of a prosperous future,
taking them to a Promised Land.

On a wing
a dream
a government invitation
to see the mother country
where some were stationed in the war.

Citizen enough for war.
Citizen enough for work,
but citizen enough to call it home?

Jamaica sailed to sea-sea-sea
for the motherland's prosperity
for all that they could see-see-see
was the bottom of the great blue?

The inflamed speeches of Powell,
Thatcher's swamping fears,
sudden amnesia to the fact of a people's
invite here.

You put your whole self in,
you put your whole self out,
in
out
in
out
you shake it all about,
criticism from the left
scapegoated by the right
but, don't forget your invite
R.S.V.P
A.S.A.P

Men measured travel time in
cigarette rollups
before the face of a new fear,
behind smiles that smouldered
their response diagnosed as a chip on the shoulder.

I wonder
how liquid brown eyes
met with the signs for;
NO Coloureds
NO Irish
NO dogs,
how a man warmed at all
in the shawl of a culture shock,
another sleeps with his pulse
on his mothers photo.
A keepsake of home,
safe
under the pillow.

The Forecast

Transparency, reveals dismal south-easterly
and rising. Variation, unseeable.
Mother's tears at first, Joy.
Then showers - not so good.

Lightening in the front room:
the tv set casting
black and white across
the glass ceiling.

Dogger of the sitting-room armchair – increasing.
Voice Boomer. Cromarty, veering china shatterer.
Later cyclonic when 5.00 – 6.00.
Demanding tea on the table, 7.00 – 8.00.
If not, wall decoration Jackson Pollock.

Iron tones radiate, falling North.
8.05, Scilly high pressure lecture
on time and its importance. Midnight.
Depression association: Humble at first.
Malice. Then, Crocodile regret,
Self-evident.

Viking strategy, outdated
such presence needed
like a light-vessel automatic
through the head
or a White Portland Plymouth in the eye.
Future
moderate and falling.

Locally poor.
Playing Pharaoh's daughter
on a tower block corner. Childhood is a
blood red gobstopper, spat out, it rolls south
where urban tarmac swaps rushes for bushes.
New hands find
a moon for a pocket. Chakra - a ball
to bounce on the brick road
Lucas calm. Fair Isle. Fastnet. Tomorrow.

May I wish you goodnight?
May you all keep well, and
do sleep tight.

TLC Street (page 9)

I visited New York in August 1999. It was my first and long awaited visit, and has proved to be a major inspiration, culturally and creatively to my work and life. I was captivated by what one taxi driver I met summed up as 'the beauty and beast of a city'. The contradiction of New York was also its fascination. It seemed ironic, in this buzzing metropolis known for its love and praise of all things commercial, that a street's name reminded people of the simpler, deeper, tender things in life.

Mother: Daughter (Page 11)

This piece was written as part of a commission for Leeds City Voice Literature Festival. The commission required that the relationship between reading as inspiration for writing be explored and a piece of existing work be utilised as the starting point of inspiration for new work. The piece explores some of the more complex elements of my identity as a woman of mixed parentage: African and white English. I read Jackie Kay's book *The Adoption Papers* and was inspired at the poetic dialogue between daughter, birth mother and adoptive mother. I decided to write a piece from the perspective of a birth mother and daughter.

Moveable Type (Page 31)

The book's title has meaning which is threefold. Firstly it is a reference to the theme of journeying and travel which underpins the book. Secondly to the political and at times emotional nature of the subject matter. Thirdly, it refers to the type of mechanical printing that emerged, initially in China in the eleventh century. The credit for manufacturing Moveable Type is given to Johann Gutenberg in the fifteenth century. The process involved the creation of a system of metal reliefs of letters organised on to a frame. The development of Moveable Type is associated with freedom of speech and opportunity for greater democratic thought. . The mass production of books and the ability to produce them quicker meant ideas could be disseminated to a larger, wider audience.

The Trace of James Brown's Scream (page 44)

James Brown is the most sampled artist in recording history. Due to the rate of James Brown samples integrated into tracks without royalty payment to the artist, there are individuals employed to seek out used samples and due payment. One of the most famous of Brown's samples is his hallmark scream. It seems a strange twist then that James Brown has spent time in prison for assault against his wife.

Salted Grin (Page 58)

When I first heard the folk song *He Moved Through The Fair* I spoke to the singer afterwards and was told it was a love song. My perception of it was more disturbing than that. I decided to write a poem inspired by the initial imagery of the piece, but which expanded and explored the more violent aspects of the original song.